JAMES C. RICHARDS

# BETTER *is* BETTER

CLASSIC DAY
PUBLISHING

Requests for such permissions should be addressed to:
Classic Day Publishing
2925 Fairview Avenue East
Seattle, Washington 98102
877-728-8837
www.classicdaypub.com

For additional copies of *Better is Better*
and more information on James C. Richards
go to www.jamescrichards.com

# DEDICATION

This book is dedicated to George Evans, who was my first mentor in the field of advising others about their finances. He taught me an immense amount about how we, as people, think about our money and what we can do with it. George's life was full of more triumphs and trials than most of us will ever experience, and he always had great stories that he would tell to make his point about something he wanted to explain. This would drive me nuts because I just wanted a quick answer. George forced me to understand more about the question, so that I could realize that there was not _one_ answer, but rather an answer specific to each person. One of his favorite sayings was "More is _not_ better; better is better, and if you want to help your clients you need to figure out what better is for _them_." From that saying comes the title of this book. George is gone now, and I dearly miss him, but perhaps through this effort some of his wisdom will live on.

James C. Richards – January 23, 2010

# Introduction

This is a book about making decisions. We all make decisions every day, but often we don't really know *why* we decided something the way we did. For many of life's decisions, such as "cream in your coffee?" decision making is based on personal preference, and that's perfectly fine. But financial decisions have an enormous impact on our lives, and I believe that far too often we make them based on the erroneous concept that *More is Better.*

The idea that *More is Better* is simply a default that we return to if we can't come up with anything else, and, because many people never try to come up with anything else, they just stick with that and call it good. I like to challenge my clients to think about what really is *Better* for them, and *sometimes* their answer *is* more! Most times, however, once they truly ponder the topic, they realize that they want certain changes to occur in their lives; while more money may help bring those changes about, just having more money by itself won't actually make their lives *Better.*

I wrote this book because I have found that *Better is Better* is a very rewarding way to think for both my clients and myself. Even though I have been talking to people about how their money affects their lives for many years, I wanted to share these ideas with a broader audience. I hope the concepts in this book help you to make your life *Better*.

Now a disclaimer: This book is not meant to tell you exactly what you should do regarding your financial situation. The purpose of this book is to have you consider a *new way of thinking* so that you can effectively do the following:

1. Clearly define what *Better* means for you.

2. Consider what changes in your life will move you closer to your definition of *Better*.

3. Evaluate your resources (income, holdings, abilities, relationships) based on how they help you achieve your definition of *Better*.

4. Start making your financial decisions based on *Better is Better*.

# Table of contents

# Section One:

The problem we face – a way to break it down into manageable pieces, and a method for making good decisions

# You have *More,* why isn't your life *Better*?

In June, 1965, I was 2 years old, and, while I don't recall it happening, the Rolling Stones released their album with the hit single "(I can't get no) Satisfaction." In the years since, it has become truly iconic. Many people around the world can certainly hum the melody if not actually sing a fair number of the words. The song has become a part of the lexicon of our society, and in 2006 it was added to the Library of Congress National Recording Registry. But in the 45 years since a very young Mick Jagger belted out those words, we still haven't gotten much closer to satisfaction. Why not?

We certainly have more in terms of quantity. The average household income in the United States is now about *eight times* what it was in 1965. Back then, only about one out of every five households had a TV, and they were almost all black & white. Now, it is hard to find a household that doesn't have two or three TVs. We have more electronics, bigger houses, faster cars, an almost limitless array of entertainment, and so much more food that obesity is a national problem. Yet we don't feel *Better*.

Could it be that more does <u>*not*</u> create better? We had a few lessons growing up that suggested that it didn't (more beer, more of those green apples, more toys than we could play with at birthdays), but we assumed those were exceptions because it just makes sense…more IS better, right? Well, not necessarily.

I believe that *Better is Better*. In addition, it is my experience that the definition of *Better* is unique to each person and that a large majority of people have never stopped to think about what their definition of *Better* might be. Were the Rolling Stones right? Is satisfaction unobtainable? I don't think so, but after nearly 20 years of talking with people about their money I have noticed a few themes:

1. Many people do not fully appreciate how much their quality of life is affected by the decisions they make regarding their money.

2. Without even knowing it, people are using a collection of conventional wisdom, other people's ideas, and rules of thumb to make critical financial decisions.

3. With the increasing complexity inherent in most financial decisions, many people are confused and overwhelmed, so they just default to a *More is Better* decision model.

4. The problems inherent in the first three themes combine to create a lot of stress and a feeling of real frustration. We all do our best to make the right decisions, but satisfaction seems out of reach.

A perfect example of this happened a few years ago when a woman came to see me looking for some financial help. She was very concerned and upset about her 401(k) plan and other accounts earmarked for retirement; she wanted to know if she had the money in the right allocations. With the *Better is Better* concept in mind, I told her I needed to know what her plans for retirement were. She hemmed and hawed and didn't seem clear on what she wanted. To help her get thinking, I said something along the lines of, *"Think about at what age you want to retire. Do you want to live in the house you live in now, or do you want to move to a retirement community? Do you plan to travel? Where are your children? Will you visit them often? Are there specific activities that you want to pursue?"*

She thought for a while, and I assumed she was imagining playing with grandchildren on the beach or golfing in Arizona. Instead, she said, *"I never want to be a bag lady. I see these women with their shopping carts piled high with their meager and tattered belongings, trying to stay dry under the freeway overpass out of the rain. They are dirty, cold, and hunched over with this sort of vacant look in their eyes; it scares me to death that I might one day be like that."*

Clearly, she had thought of this before! For this woman, security and stability have immensely more value than just "more money." No wonder she was so worried and conflicted. Without stopping to consider what was most important to her, she had been following conventional wisdom that said she should set up her 401(k) for maximum growth, and every time the market went down she envisioned her future self under an overpass, cold and hungry, with all of her possessions in a shopping cart! The decisions she had made about her retirement accounts were having a profound effect on her quality of life every single day, and she was using the wrong assumptions to make her choices.

There are many examples of this type of default thinking:

- My mother always told me to pay off the mortgage as fast as I could.

- I can't sell this holding, because I'll have to pay taxes on the gain.

- Debt is bad; I do everything in cash.

- I'm going to retire in 3 years; I should have all my money in bonds and cash.

- I'm young; I should put all my savings in a 401(k) and make it very aggressive.

- This stuff is confusing; I'll just pick the default choice.

- *More is Better.*

Let me be very clear: the above statements are not inherently wrong. The point I want to make is that these ideas or ones like them may be part of your decision model but they do not result in a higher quality of life *for you*. Chances are good you don't even consciously know you are using these ideas in your decision model, but they still have a significant impact on your long-term well-being and your day-to-day stress level, and they often create a vague sense of dissatisfaction.

The notion that *More* is *Better* is ingrained in us. It may even be some sort of primal notion going back to our ancient ancestors who were on the hunt. Clearly, for them, a bigger mammoth was better than a smaller one. However, evolving has its advantages, and one of them is having the ability to actually think and make rational decisions rather than just acting on instinct. In this book we are going to explore a solution to combat this "default thinking" and look at ways in which you can determine what the foundations of your decision model really should be. Then you can start making decisions that result in a higher quality of life—decisions that will make your life *Better*.

## SUMMARY

1. Our quality of life is deeply affected by the decisions we make regarding our money.

2. We often make critical financial decisions using a "default" decision model that is full of ideas that may apply to somebody else, but may not apply to us.

3. The result of "default" decision making is a sense of frustration and dissatisfaction.

4. The definition of *Better* is unique to each individual, but many people have not defined what *Better* really means to them.

Regardless of where they come from or how true they were for someone else, we have many preconceptions firmly embedded in us that do not really apply to our unique situation. One of the most dangerous to our long-term well-being is the idea that *More is Better*.

# CHAPTER 2

# What can you really do with your money?

Finances are complicated, and they are getting more so every day. They can easily become overwhelming, and when that happens people usually say something like, "The heck with it, I don't know what to do, I'll just do what my friend/brother/parents did." To try to avoid the mental overload that comes with a high level of complexity and give you the chance to think about what *you* really want, let's start with a framework that keeps things simple.

One of the best parts of my job is that I have some wonderful clients who always make me think. A woman came to my office one day, and, after we got to know each other a little, she said:

*"Our family has always had money, but frankly I have been totally disinterested in anything to do with it. Now I have to grow up and start paying attention, so could you tell me ALL of the options I have for my money?"*

I responded, "*ALL of the options?*"

She had her notepad ready and was looking for a long list. "*Yes. I'd like to know about all my choices for what to do with my money.*"

I thought about it for a while and then replied, "*Well, really there are only three options.*"

She looked at me as if I must be some sort of simpleton and probably started thinking that perhaps she'd gone to the wrong office. "*There must be more than that: checking, savings, mutual funds, stocks, bonds, CDs, real estate. I just named seven without even trying very hard.*"

I responded, "*Those are all places where you can _keep_ your money, but there are only three things you can _do_ with your money. Those three things are: spend it, save it, or give it away.*" This woman was jumping ahead to where to _keep_ her money so that it could grow, without giving any thought to what she was actually trying to _do_ with it.

For many people, the subject of money and how you use it in your life can be totally overwhelming and confusing. It helps to realize that anything you are doing with your money is some form of these three options. While those three basic options are the core, sometimes they overlap, and so to help clients simplify their financial lives I expanded the three core areas to five separate categories that are cleanly distinct from each other:

- **Spend it** on basic needs, possessions, experiences, and help

- Both **Spend and Save it** to create security

- **Save it** for a future spending need

- **Give it** to the government by paying taxes

- **Give it** to charity

For each one of these five categories, there is a right way and a wrong way to go about using your money, and what follows is a description and a general guideline for each category. Then, in Chapter 3, we are going to work on your personal decision model, which will guide you on how to make decisions specific to your definition of *Better*.

## Spend it on basic needs, possessions, experiences, and help

When we are doing planning, I often ask clients how much money they need to live each month. I also ask them how much they make a year. Most of the time, they don't really know the answer to either question! Life is busy, and not everyone likes to keep all the receipts and add everything up, so many people just spend what they need to and check the balance at the ATM and hope it stays above zero. We spend money all the time, but we're often too busy to give it a lot of thought.

We have to spend part of our money just to exist. We pay rent or the mortgage so that we have a place to rest at night, we buy food so that we don't go hungry, we buy clothes for warmth, and so forth. Some people call this a "monthly nut" — fixed expenses, or the basic cost of living. For a large part of the world's population, this basic amount is certainly not a given, and to have excess is very unlikely. But, if you are reading this, you are probably blessed with being somewhat financially stable, and this part of your budget has become rather automatic. What happens with the money remaining after these basic necessities have been paid for is where things can get interesting.

You can just spend whatever is left, and, in fact, you can spend a whole lot more than that, thanks to credit cards and easy financing for major purchases. Many people do this after getting their first real job. The paycheck is bigger than they have ever seen before, and they *feel* rich. They immediately spend what seem like little amounts here and there. "*I just got a $1,000 pay check, so this new phone for $300 is a no brainer!*" Pretty soon, however, they find out that the "little" things add up very quickly, frequently leaving them with credit card debt. Hopefully, they pay off the debt, learn their lesson, and move on, but many people never do. They keep buying things they *think* will make them happy, the debt keeps piling up, the stress builds, and in the end they are miserable and can't figure out why. By using the credit card and paying all the interest and feeling all the stress they gave up a lot of resources (purchase price, interest, mental energy), and what did they get? Oftentimes, they can't even tell you what they got! I would argue that they did not trade resources to make their life *Better*.

The point I want to make about spending is that there is an exchange—you are letting go of some of your money in order to get something in return. That something might be a tangible item, such as a TV; an experience, such as a movie; or a service, such as having your car washed, but, in the end, you expect to receive something in return for your money. The guideline for spending is: **Determine what you are going to receive** in the exchange and what it is really going to cost you, and then ask yourself, "Will this trade make my life *Better*?"

## Spend and Save it to create security

Security is the ability to handle life's problems. If you get laid off, security means you have money in savings to pay the bills while you find another job. If you become ill, it might mean good medical insurance. For many of us, having savings in the bank just for a "rainy day" makes us feel better because we know we can make it through a difficult time of life without giving up too much quality of life. How much is enough? That depends.

The concept of security has different value to different people. My wife and I have a 13-year-old son named Ben. When I suggested that he should save some of his birthday money, he looked at me like I had two heads! (Actually that isn't all that unusual, teenagers being what they are.) He really didn't like the idea at all; to him, saving money seems to make as much sense as doing extra math homework just for fun. He can't imagine anything good that will result because he saved the money, and his life experience backs up that opinion. Up to this point in his life, his parents have provided everything he needs in the way of food, clothing, and shelter, although I suppose he might argue that we have not provided enough cell phones, video games, and junk food. When it comes down to it, however, he knows he won't starve if he spends all of his birthday money on loading his iPod® with reruns of *The Simpsons*™. But not everyone sees life that way. The woman from Chapter 1 who was worried about becoming a bag lady puts much more value on security than does my 13-year-old son!

Most of us like at least a little "cushion"—a savings account with some emergency money is a basic tenet of financial planning—but there is no way we can always have enough money in savings to cover any problem that might come our way. That is where insurance comes into play. We can create security in a different way by spending money on insurance and knowing that someone else will cover us if something big happens. The guideline for security is: **Define what level of security is *Better* for you and then design the combination of savings and insurance that makes you most comfortable.**

## Save it for future spending

Back before easy payment plans and credit cards, people saved up their money for a large purchase like a piece of furniture or a car. They did not buy something they could not pay for, and that is still a pretty good way to go. Debt certainly does have its place in a good financial plan, especially for items that would be very difficult to save enough money to pay for all at once, such as a house, an education, or tools to start a business. But for discretionary items such as dinners, clothes, and toys of all kinds, having the money before you spend it will create less stress and make your life *Better*.

In addition to having money for discretionary items, most of us would like to get to the point where we do not *need* to work, so retirement is easily the largest future spending goal most people have. Others include paying for college for children, or taking a big vacation. Sometimes you don't even know what your future spending might be. I urge my clients to save some money in an "opportunity fund." We don't know what that money will be spent on, because life is ever-changing, but over the years I have seen many situations in which an opportunity fund made something possible that no one had thought of in advance.

Saving for future spending is an area where some people fall into the *More is Better* trap. There is a balance to be struck between saving for later and quality of life right now, such as between getting all the tax savings on retirement plans versus having money for a family vacation.

I once went to a wedding: he was 74, she was 72. Both of their previous spouses had died of cancer a few years before. As I sat watching the wedding, my mind wandered to the two spouses that had passed away. How much quality of life did they give up to save for a retirement that never happened? Immediately after the reception, I called the travel agent and upgraded my upcoming vacation to first class! I doubt my retirement will be much different, and we had a great time on vacation. As with all things in life, moderation is the key: don't live all for the moment, but don't go overboard on saving for the future either.

The guideline for savings is: **Establish goals that are *Better* for you, but be sure they don't reduce quality of life in another area.**

## Give it to the government by paying taxes

No one I've ever met likes paying taxes, but we pay them because no one I've ever met likes jail either. However, we do have some control over how *much* we pay in taxes.

In a court case many years ago the judge stated: *"Anyone may arrange his affairs so that his taxes shall be as low as possible; he is not bound to choose that pattern which best pays the treasury. There is not even a patriotic duty to increase one's taxes. Over and over again the Courts have said that there is nothing sinister in so arranging affairs as to keep taxes as low as possible. Everyone does it, rich and poor alike and all do right, for nobody owes any public duty to pay more than the law demands: Taxes are enforced exactions, not voluntary contributions. To demand more in the name of morals is mere cant."*—**Honorable Learned Hand, U.S. Appeals Court Judge,** *Helvering v. Gregory*, 69 F.2d 809 (1934).

How do you "arrange affairs so that taxes shall be as low as possible"? You take the time to find out what the tax impact of a certain action is and then make your decision. For example, you can choose to live in a different city with a lower property tax rate, you can choose one investment over another because one creates less tax, and, rather than invest in a regular account, you can put money in a formal retirement plan that provides a tax deduction. I would not suggest making decisions based *solely* on the tax angle, but by keeping the tax impact in mind we can use the *Better is Better* approach to reduce the amount of taxes we pay and then redirect that money to areas that are more important to us. This is tax avoidance; it is completely legal, and Judge Hand implied it is what any prudent person would do. Tax *evasion* is a very different matter; it is where you purposely lie to reduce your taxes. It is quite illegal, and the IRS agents might show up to chat with you about it should you pursue that option. Many of the 20th century mobsters were incarcerated not for murder, extortion, or racketeering, but for tax evasion. It's serious stuff, and I absolutely do not recommend it.

The goal for this category of what you can do with your money is simple: **Pay all of the taxes you legally owe and not one penny more!**

## Give it to charity

I said that when you spend money you ideally trade it for something that makes your life better, and when you keep it you create security, so if you are trying to make

<u>your</u> life *Better* why in the world would you give your money away? Because *More* isn't necessarily *Better*, and *Better* comes in a variety of flavors.

Almost everyone has been asked to give away some of their money. The requests can come from a capital campaign at your college, a fundraiser at your house of worship, or the person with a sign at the freeway off-ramp. There is an innate part of us that makes us uncomfortable if we know someone is suffering or needs our help and that causes us to want to take some form of action. Once we have considered the request we might not take any action, either because we think someone else will do it or because we believe the request is a scam or that we are unable to help, but the idea that helping others is a good thing to do is a pretty basic part of the human condition. I have been asking clients about their feelings around philanthropy for many years, and I have never gotten exactly the same answer as to where they give and why. The answers range from "I want to give it all away" to "I don't want to give any at all," and it is a deeply personal concept. For those that do give, I believe that they do it because they feel it is the right thing to do, because it gives them joy to see those they helped, and because it feeds their souls.

For those that enjoy it, giving away money is a wonderful thing to do, but it should be done correctly. How could money be given away incorrectly? You could create a support system that is so comfortable for people that they never learn to take care of themselves. You could give money to an organization that uses 80% of its revenue to pay the staff and only 20% on the specific cause. You could overwhelm a small grassroots group with a gift too big for them to manage. In Chapter 8 we'll explore more about giving so that the desired end result is most likely to happen, but in general the goal for this category is: **Give to charities that support your version of *Better*, and do so in a way that has the greatest impact.**

## SUMMARY

Keep it simple. There are just five things to do with money and each one has a basic goal:

1. **Spend it:** Determine what you are going to receive in the exchange and what it is really going to cost you and then ask yourself, "Will this trade make my life *Better*?"

2. **Use it to create security:** Define what level of security is *Better* for you and then design the combination of savings and insurance that fits that goal.

3. **Save it for future spending:** Establish savings goals that are *Better* for you, but be sure they don't reduce your quality of life in another area.

4. **Pay taxes:** Pay all of the taxes you legally owe and not one penny more!

5. **Give it to charity:** Give to charities that support your version of *Better*, and do so in a way that has the greatest impact.

# CHAPTER 3

# To achieve *Better,* you have to know what it is

Parents of teenagers know all about the word "whatever." It's just a word, right? It can be used in a lovely manner, such as "whatever you'd like, dear." But in the hands (or vocal cords) of a teenager it is used as a singularity. It stands alone in all its glory. It has power. In three artfully enunciated syllables it conveys an encyclopedia worth of disdain, revulsion, and indifference. The real art form is in how they present those three syllables—WHAT-evvvvvvvv-er, Whaaaaat-ev-errrr, What-EV-er. Spoken in almost any accent, volume, or tone the word is nearly guaranteed to annoy parents, which is exactly the point.

I tell you about this to set the stage for a great example of homing in on what is important to a person. Imagine, if you will, a 15-year-old, snooty, all-about-me teenage girl. She's perfect for this example, because kids at this age are typically in the "all about *me*" mindset. We can talk to her, but we won't get any real response until we get to something that *she* thinks is important.

**Jim:** Your grandfather gave you some preferred stock.

**Her:** (eyes roll) What-evvvvvvv-er.

**Jim:** It's a good company with a long track record of dividends.

**Her:** (hair flip) Whaaat-ev-eeeeeeer.

**Jim:** The dividends have an annual rate of nearly 5%.

**Her:** (freshens lipstick) What-ev-r.

**Jim:** We could set up an auto-sweep of dividends on a quarterly basis.

**Her:** (texts to friend: **OMG old gys r weird**) Whaaaat-evvvvvvvvvvvvvvvvv-errrrrrrrr.

**Jim:** This would put more money in your checking account, and you could buy things.

**Her:** (raises eyebrow) Whatever.

**Jim:** Weren't you wanting the latest cool shoes that all your friends have, but they were too expensive?

**Her:** Yeah, so?

**Jim:** Well, if the dividends from your grandfather's gift were put into your checking account, you would have the money to buy the shoes.

**Her:** (head snaps around, eyes focus) OK, I'm listening, what should I do?

See my point? She only really cared about the conversation when we got down to what really mattered *to her*.

## Discovering what matters to you

So what matters to you? What *really* matters? What gets you to stop saying "*whatever*" and start paying attention? That can sometimes be difficult to figure out. The things that matter most are typically the things that you feel at a "gut" level or have very base emotions about. Love, hate, greed, and fear—these are all deep, base emotions, and they will give us some good guidance as to what really matters to you.

Our personal priorities should be easy to figure out if they are so meaningful, right? It seems natural that we would be able to easily list them, because these ideas are very central to who we are. The problem is that what you find important can become covered up with "noise": programming your new phone, appointments, oil changes, job deadlines, and 100 other bits of daily life that effectively camouflage what is really important to you. These core values don't go away; they are always there, but if we find ourselves ignoring them the result is a vague sense of dissatisfaction. In order to get down to what really matters we have to move some of the clutter out of the way for a bit.

In our practice, when my clients enter our conference room they are basically stuck there with me and no other distractions. (Some like that better than others!) I then ask a very simple question to help clients unearth what really matters to them: "How can I help?" The question is hardly rocket science, but it is effective. The combination of being away from all the distractions and having permission to talk about whatever they want usually gets us down to the meaningful issues in a hurry. If not, I get a bit more focused on those base emotions: What do you love in life? What annoys you most? What scares you most? What keeps you awake at night? The answers are always there, but usually a bit hidden in life's clutter.

Sometimes the answers show up at the back door while you are looking out the front. I rarely hear "I don't know," but I do hear things that suggest a broader meaning. For example, one new client replied by saying, "The reason I am here is that everything I have is scattered about in a number of places. I don't even really know what I have, let alone where it is. I have this shopping bag of unopened statements [yes, someone really said that to me once], and I'm just not sure what I need."

On the surface that sounds like "I don't know," but the answer is there. This is a person who does not enjoy keeping track of things and wants life simplified. They want someone to sort things out, get information in one place, and, if possible, send them a single statement. What is really important to this person is *simplicity*. For someone like this, we would design a very simple plan. We know that, over time, it may be possible to make more money by adding some complexity, but if we did that we would fall into the trap of *More is Better*. For this person, *Better* equals simple, clear, and easy to manage. To know which course of action is *Better for you*, we have to know what really matters *to you*.

## Defining the Four Foundations

Even if you aren't trapped in a conference room letting me ask you questions, you can still discover what is truly important to you, it just takes a little more effort. The following exercise is a great way to zero in on those issues. However, because I'm not going to lock you in a room, it is critical that you choose a quiet environment where you can focus on the task at hand. Do not try to do it in a coffee shop, while fighting rush hour traffic, or in an airport. Find a private spot where it is just you and your pad of paper. Turn off the phone, close your e-mail, and ensure that you have 30–45 minutes to do this. I am certain you will find the time well spent.

On your paper, make a table like the one below:

| I LOVE | I HATE | I WANT | I FEAR |
|--------|--------|--------|--------|
|        |        |        |        |
|        |        |        |        |
|        |        |        |        |
|        |        |        |        |
|        |        |        |        |

You might recognize the pattern: the headings are our deep core emotions—love, hate, greed, and fear. Wait, greed? How do you use greed to make your life *Better*? Michael Douglas made the line "greed is good" famous in the movie *Wall Street*, but the statement goes against everything our parents drilled into us as kids, so it feels wrong to talk about greed in any sort of positive fashion. For my purpose, I just accept that it is an emotion we all have, and, like the other emotions, it is just fine when it is kept in balance. If you had no fear, you'd burn your hands on the stove, walk in front of cars, and generally fail to survive. Too much fear results in a person who can't leave home or get out of bed. Greed is similar:

too little and you will starve to death, too much and you will likely end up in prison. A certain amount of desire to have more is pretty healthy. In order to make the whole exercise flow better, I have changed the term "greed" to "I want." Also, it is helpful when we think about these deep emotions to note that love and hate are about things that already exist; want and fear are about things that could be.

Here are some clarifications that may help you as you fill in the table:

**I LOVE:** These are things that you really care about. They may be experiences, people, places, possessions, or an abstract concept, such as security, flexibility, or control. For the most part you already have them.

**I HATE:** These are things that detract from a better life. They, too, may be experiences, people, places, possessions, or an abstract concept, like security, flexibility, or control. Like the items that you love, they are in your life now.

**I WANT:** These are similar to the items in the I LOVE column. However, these are the things that you would like to see in your life but don't have now.

**I FEAR:** These are things that *could happen*, and if they did, your quality of life would be reduced, usually in a pretty dramatic way.

Fill in the boxes with whatever comes to mind, but keep in mind that your answers should be fairly broad topics. I hate tomato juice in my beer, but that fact isn't going to get me very far with my finances. Try to fill in all 20 boxes if you can, but only if the responses are truly meaningful to you. It is better to have three that are "core" than five that are only mildly meaningful to you. You are now looking at a pretty strong snapshot of what is really important to you. Here's an example:

| I LOVE | I HATE | I WANT | I FEAR |
|---|---|---|---|
| My family | Stress over money | To increase literacy rates in the 3rd world | Not being able to provide for my family |
| Airplanes | Wasting time | To be able to pay my kid's college costs | Being a burden to my kids |
| Friendships | Complexity | To learn to play an instrument | Climate change |
| Living near water | Being overscheduled | Simplicity in my life | Losing part of my nest egg |
| Flexibility | Record keeping | To work 4 days a week | Being a bag lady |

Now, take those four columns and translate them into something that you can use to guide your financial decisions. These Four Foundations will direct you in how to work toward achieving what is *Better* for you.

### From the I LOVE Column

Write a statement that says, "I am going to make financial decisions so that my life is *Better* because I have *more* _____"; fill in the blank with themes from your I LOVE column.

### From the I HATE Column

Write a statement that says, "I am going to make financial decisions so that my life is *Better* because I have *less* _____"; fill in the blank with themes from your I HATE column.

### From the I WANT Column

Write a statement that says, "I am going to make financial decisions so that my life is *Better* because I *will be able to* _____"; fill in the blank with themes from your I WANT column.

### From the I FEAR Column

Write a statement that says, "I am going to make financial decisions so that my life is *Better* because I have taken steps to *reduce my concern about* _____"; fill in the blank with themes from your I FEAR column.

From the example, the Four Foundations might look like this:

- I am going to make financial decisions so that my life is *Better* because I have <u>*more*</u> time with my family and friends, the ability to spend time in and around airplanes, and a job that allows me to maintain flexibility in my schedule.

- I am going to make financial decisions so that my life is *Better* because I have <u>*less*</u> stress over money, my schedule is less hectic, and my affairs are less complex and easier to track.

- I am going to make financial decisions so that my life is *Better* because I <u>*will be able to*</u> pay my children's college costs, take Fridays off to work on literacy programs, and have the time to take music lessons.

- I am going to make financial decisions so that my life is *Better* because I have taken steps to <u>*reduce my concern about*</u> becoming a burden to my kids. I also want to have a plan in place to take care of my family if something happens to me, and I will try to reduce my carbon footprint to help combat climate change.

Now that you have your Four Foundations, you can use them as a guide when making almost any financial decision, as well as a lot of non-financial decisions. As you are pondering whether to invest in a financial opportunity, reflect on your Four Foundations and whether the opportunity supports them. At some point while judging if the opportunity aligns with your Four Foundations, the decision will often become a "no-brainer." This opportunity *might* make you more money, but if it goes directly against what you feel makes your life *Better*, then don't do it. Does that mean that it's a bad investment? No, not at all; it is a bad investment *for you* because it does not support what is really important *to you*.

## SUMMARY

1. You must understand what *Better* means to you.

2. It may not be obvious; life's clutter often hides what is really meaningful.

3. You can discover what is *Better* for you by exploring four base emotions: love, hate, greed, and fear.

4. You can write out your Four Foundation statements and then use those statements to guide your financial decisions toward what is *Better* for you.

Once you know what *Better* is for you, you can make *Better* decisions.

# Section Two:

Applying the solution method to the five basic uses for your money

# CHAPTER 4

# Spending money now so you really enjoy it

A client came to a meeting one day holding a few shopping bags from the local mall. I inquired if she'd found anything fun or if she had just been shopping for necessities. She answered, "Oh I was just a bit down, so I decided to do a little *retail therapy*." What a great expression! But what was enjoyable about it for her? Was it the act of removing the bills from her wallet? Was it the thrill of sliding the credit card through the machine? Probably not. What I think was enjoyable for her was the acquisition of something that she perceived would make her life *Better* in some way, such as a new outfit to wear to an upcoming dinner—life would be *Better* because she would look great at the dinner and feel more confident. Or it could have been a gift for a friend's birthday—life would be *Better* because she did something nice for a friend.

Basically, we spend money with the expectation that doing so will make life *Better* in some way. What's tragic is that a fair amount of the time we give up the money, but don't get the desired result. Why is that?

## Know what you want and be sure you're going to get it

The advertising industry is a multimillion dollar machine trying to convince you that spending money on a certain product will create a certain result that *you will love*. The methods are very subtle, and, with hundreds of years of experience, the advertisers are very, very good at this. Here's an example:

Most parents wish their teens wanted to spend more time with them, would talk with them, and would think that Mom and Dad are cool (or at least not embarrassing). However, teenagers are supposed to spread their wings and look for independence. Because the teen years are a transition from dependence to independence, a harmonious family experience is unlikely at best, but parents still *want it*. Therefore, many advertisers show their products as part of a really happy family. The message goes something like this: *Buy a new five-person phone plan with XYZ cell phone provider. You'll have unlimited family calling, and your kids will love you; they will call you all of the time, do all of their homework, never be out past curfew, and take out the trash whenever you ask them to.* Clearly all of that isn't said, but it is implied by the use of images that show a happy family on the couch or romping in their lush backyard together. Without much thought, you might buy the five-person phone plan with the expectation that it would make your life *Better* by stopping any family arguments, and you would be very disappointed when that didn't happen. Most people aren't even aware they are disappointed with the results; they simply feel vaguely unfulfilled, and so they go do a little "*retail therapy*" and start the whole cycle all over again.

Sometimes the opposite happens; we *don't* spend money, because we think we shouldn't. We say, "It's a waste, we don't *really need* that, it would be extravagant." That can be the right approach, but when *Better* is the goal, sometimes spending the money *is* the right thing to do. I grew up in a basic California ranch-style house, with a big backyard. The kitchen sink faced the backyard, and above the sink was a window. My mother liked the arrangement because she could do something in the kitchen and still see what we kids were doing in the backyard. However, she hated the actual window. It had some scratches on it, it wouldn't open correctly, and there was a blind spot that kept her from seeing the entire yard. But being a practical, thrifty woman, she would not replace a perfectly good window. Instead, she arranged the kids playing baseball in such a way that the window would likely get broken! For years, she kept hoping that a high fastball would connect in a stunning line drive and smash that window to bits. It never happened (which might shine some light on why I work in personal finance, not as a baseball player).

When they went to sell the house after almost 40 years, a group came in to "stage" the house and make it look a bit more modern, to appeal to younger buyers. One of the first things they did was to change out that window; it took them about four hours and about $500. My mother was not happy! All those years she had hated that window, and the fix was so simple, and relatively cheap. Had she spent a little money back in 1970, she could have enjoyed that window for 30 years; instead, she enjoyed it for about 30 *days*, until the house sold.

You can see that *Better* doesn't just result from spending money nor does it come just from *not* spending any money. To really make progress, you have to know what you are going to receive in exchange for your money and then see if that will move you closer to your definition of *Better*. What you will receive in exchange will be possessions, experiences, help, or some combination of the three, but will the exchange make your life *Better*? If you are having a hard time deciding, refer back to your Four Foundations.

## Possessions: More stuff!

Possessions aren't as simple as they seem. Like money, they don't really have much value just sitting there. It is what they do for us or how they make our life *Better* that really gives them any meaning. One of my friends loves technology and is usually up on the latest electronic devices. He spent money on an iPhone® when they first came out, and he loved it. He had so much fun learning all the new apps—GPS tracking, music recognition, pictures, and so forth. Now the phone was just a collection of circuits, LEDs, and plastic, so just sitting on the counter it wasn't really that exciting. But for him, it provided great enjoyment because it enabled him to spend time on one of his passions—technology. His wife, on the other hand, hates cell phones in general, doesn't really want anything to do with them, and only grudgingly carries one because she has kids and the school may call. For her, there is absolutely no joy whatsoever in new smartphone technology. There you have it — same money, same phone, same circuits, same LEDs and plastic, but totally different quality of life increase/decrease depending on who has the possession.

Buying possessions can be a very good use of money, but you need to be sure that the possession is really going to increase *your* quality of life. Will an $800 purse do that? Not for me, but for one of my clients it is just the ticket! Think about what you are buying, and remember that it isn't the possession that truly matters but what effect it will have on your life. Go back and reread your Four Foundations from Chapter 3 and see if you still think that a certain possession is a great one for you to own. No matter what the advertisement says, or how many of your friends have it, or how much on sale it is, the test should be whether or not that possession will move you closer to your definition of *Better*.

## Experiences: Go out and do something

When you go to a movie, you pay your money for a ticket, go in, sit down, and watch the movie. It may make you laugh or cry, increase your heart rate, or make you examine your life. No matter what the experience is like in the theatre, when you leave you do not take any sort of possession with you. Instead you had an experience, and it changed who you are, even in a slight way. Every experience we have affects who we are, for better or for worse. If we want our life to be *Better* we should pick our experiences very carefully and understand that each experience's effect on us will last much longer than most possessions.

For many people, visiting other cultures is a great way to use their money to make their life better; for others money is well spent on movies or art exhibits, something like skydiving that gets their adrenaline pumping, or something as mellow as a picnic at the beach. Sometimes a certain possession can allow for more experiences. A view home, a camper, or a bicycle are easy examples, but one of the most fun examples I know of, once again, comes from my mother.

Mom loves spending time with her children/ grandchildren and always has at least a hundred things she wants to do at any given time. Cleaning the house is <u>not</u> one of them. Cleaning house is an activity that reduces her quality of life, and she knows it. Many years ago, we had a carpet that was nice but "showed the dirt." This translated into Mom's vacuuming more often, which translated into less time doing what she wanted to do. So she went outside with a plastic bag and gathered handfuls of dirt from all around our house, shook them all up, and went to the carpet store. She told the salesman to match the carpet to the dirt! She and my father spent money on new carpet (a possession), but mom vacuumed less and chased us kids more (an experience), and her life was *Better*.

In my life I have seen that the value of the experiences we have far outweighs that of the possessions we accumulate. When you are considering how to spend money in a way that will be *Better* for you, I strongly suggest you consider more experiences and fewer possessions.

## Help: Sometimes the best person for the job is *not* you

We've all heard that money can't buy happiness, and it is true. However, it *can* remove some things that cause frustration, which enables you to focus on things that *do* bring happiness. What I'm talking about here is the concept of using some of your spending money to hire help with tasks that you either aren't good at or just don't enjoy.

My wife is a wonderful gardener, and while I do have some God-given talents, gardening is not among them. When we were first married, she handled most of the yard work because she loved doing it. However, she saw pushing the heavy lawnmower around the hilly yard as more of a "husband chore," so mowing the lawn was on my list. I was OK with that, but I never enjoyed doing it and could easily think of many other great things to do with that time. I *may* have even complained out loud about this once or twice.

For my birthday, she was casting around for a present to give to me. After deciding that I did not need another tie and that there were plenty of flying magazines already coming to the house, she decided to buy me two months of lawn care service. I was ecstatic!— partly because I've never been big on ties, but mostly because it gave me some free time. I will never forget the day that I was loading my windsurfing gear into the car when the lawn guys showed up. They hopped out of their truck, gave me a big smile, and said "Going out to play, eh?" It was an epiphany! I could pay these guys to do something that I hated, and I could go do something I loved instead! As an added bonus, they were thrilled to have the work, which enabled them to support their families. It was a win-win situation. Yes, the yard service cost money, which meant that I did not have enough money to buy a new windsurfing sail that year. But I was far happier. My life was *Better* sailing with my old sail while these guys mowed my lawn than it would have been if I had a new sail in the garage but no time to use it. I sold the mower to my neighbor and never looked back.

You have limited resources and your time is one of the most precious. Don't waste your time on doing activities that don't make your life *Better* if you have a viable alternative. For almost any activity that you don't like there is someone that does it well, wants the work, and would love to help you. When you use your money to pay for help, and use the extra time on something you want more of, you move toward *Better*.

## SUMMARY

1.  We spend money in the hopes of making our lives *Better.*

2.  Oftentimes we don't get the result we were hoping for, so it is important to really know what you are going to get and whether it will make your life *Better*.

3.  There are three things we get in exchange for spending: possessions, experiences, and help.

4.  All three have the potential to make your life *Better*, but you need to choose them wisely.

Use *Better* as a guide to which possessions to buy. Consider having more experiences and less "stuff," and, by all means, hire help. *More* is <u>not</u> *Better*; *Better* is *Better*.

# CHAPTER 5

# Using money to create the security you want

## Security

If everything was fair, if bad things only happened to bad people, if there was no such thing as "an act of God," if bubbles only existed on the soap dish instead of in real estate markets and stock markets, and if we never made a bad decision, then we *might* be able to only move forward. In some fantasy realm, those statements may be true, but here in our dimension they most certainly are not. If we want to move forward toward achieving what we individually define as *Better*, there *must* be some plans in place to avoid going backwards when things go wrong.

In 2006 a very nice couple I'd worked with for a few years asked about buying a rental house. They had read in an article that the real estate market was the latest hot thing. They did some research and said the down payment would be about $40,000, and they had most of that in savings and could borrow the rest from his 401(k).

The rent would cover all but about $200 a month of the costs; they felt they could afford the amount, and the rental would help them build their wealth. They even put together a spreadsheet showing the rent increases each year, how in five years the project would be in positive cash flow, and how much the house would appreciate. Great stuff and it really looked good.

After I studied the sheet for a while I realized something was missing; I asked, "Where is the contingency fund?" "Contingency for what?" they asked. It was a classic mistake. In their enthusiasm, they forgot to allow for the risk of a tenant failing to pay rent, the roof starting to leak, or the plumbing turning out to be not quite as perfect as the seller suggested it was. If they had completed this deal and had a $10,000 hit in the first year (which is not a very big hit when dealing with houses), they would have been in real financial trouble. Recall that they would have used all of their savings and a loan on his 401(k) for the down payment. Because Murphy's Law seems to apply in situations like this, one of them might have a job loss or some other issue, and, if so, suddenly the whole thing would collapse, taking with it their down payment, all of their hard work, and probably some additional legal costs. In order to take risk, you must have a backup plan.

When we consider the four base emotions from Chapter 3, we tend to pay more attention to what might happen (Want & Fear) than on what already exists (Love & Hate). Between those two that might happen, most people would much rather think about Want than Fear. I can get people to talk all day long about investments, but mention insurance or a will and a cold fog comes over the room. We focus on what's ahead, what we want to do next, what we want to acquire, or how we can increase our score. What we usually do not do is spend time thinking about how to avoid going backwards. Once we have something, we often assume we will always have it. Is it possible to eliminate all chances of ever going backwards? Absolutely not. So what can you do?

## Be honest about the potential danger

The first step is to be totally honest with yourself about the potential danger and what it means to you. Take the bull by the horns and look it in the eye and see how bad it is. Carefully evaluate the risk and how the loss would affect you in light of your definition of *Better*. Alfred Hitchcock was a master filmmaker, and one of his special methods for scaring people was to use their own imaginations against them. When we have a blank spot in the story, we automatically fill it in with whatever we think fits best. If you are watching a scary movie, and there is a blank spot in the story, the visual that fits best is the scariest one *you can imagine*. Mr. Hitchcock knew this. When he really wanted to scare you, he left out certain critical parts and just let your imagination do the work. This was brilliant because rather than assuming one size fits all or that one type of scene would really scare everyone, he went for customization—all people experienced real fear, because they plugged in what was most fear-inducing for them.

That's what happens to all of us when we have a vague fear of something. We imagine the worst-case scenario, which can either paralyze us with fear or cause us to simply stop evaluating whatever scares us. This is the reason I get interesting reactions when I bring up the subject of security. "I hate insurance; I just don't want to think about it." "Talking about writing a will is just creepy, let's skip that part." Or my favorite head-in-the-sand statement: "I like to think only positive thoughts." The key to reducing your stress about risks and thus making your life *Better* is to fill in the blanks with real facts, not just the worst you can imagine. Once you have a good, clear picture of what the risk really is, then you can decide what to do about it. You can make plans to eliminate or at least reduce that risk and/or transfer the risk to someone else. As long as you leave it vague, it will haunt you every day.

As to which risks to look at, I would certainly start with the items you listed in the "I Fear" column in Chapter 3, but don't necessarily stop there. You may not have put down a house fire as one of your great fears, but it is still a risk that you should address. The first step here is to ask yourself two questions about the potential event that worries you:

- Do I really need to worry about it? Some risks just aren't that big of a deal. You can probably handle the pain if the $59 printer breaks after the warranty runs out.

- Can I eliminate it? Many risks we choose to take, but don't have to. Examples might include crossing the street at a dangerous intersection instead of walking two blocks to the stoplight, or investing in a financial deal that is way out of our comfort zone.

Don't breeze by that second question; it addresses a major cause of people's lives not being *Better*. They take risks that they do not need to and in the process add a lot of stress to their lives, even if the risk doesn't go against them. Why do people take unnecessary risks? Sometimes they don't even know they are, such as when they buy into an investment they did not really understand. Sometimes it is pure greed that blinds them to the risks that are involved. Sometimes it is "peer pressure," which I can assure you applies to adults as well as kids. Often they set themselves up by taking one risk, and when that starts to go against them they must take an even bigger risk to try to get out of trouble. This sort of decision pattern usually ends in bankruptcy court.

Be very selective with which risks you choose to take, and be sure that they do not take away from what makes your life *Better*. However, if you can't eliminate a risk (or choose not to) and you feel it is big enough to make an impact in your life, then you need to *take action* in order to reduce the stress, create some security, and make your life *Better*.

## Don't worry, take action!

Worry is a total waste of mental energy. I am all for carefully considering a potential danger and planning ahead in case it happens, but to just sit and worry serves no useful purpose at all. You need to either accept that you have no control over that issue and then not worry about it or *take action*.

**Action # 1: Reduce the chance it will happen**

The steps that reduce your exposure to risk are pretty simple most of the time, they just take a little thought and possibly a change of habits. Other than the slightly crazy men and women who do Hollywood stunts, I'm pretty sure nobody wants to go through a car windshield. You could actually eliminate this risk altogether by never getting into a car, but in our society that isn't very practical. Instead, you can dramatically reduce the chance it will happen by simply wearing your seat belt every time you are in a car.

Another example is in investing. By not putting your entire portfolio in one stock you will reduce the chance of losing all your money. At home, putting smoke detectors in your house allows for early warning of a potential problem and reduces the chance of a major house fire. Health-wise, exercise and a good diet reduce the chance of heart problems. For almost every risk there are at least a few things you can do to reduce the chance of it happening, and these things are usually easy to do and fairly inexpensive. This is a great place to start making your life *Better*.

**Action # 2: Have a plan to reduce the potential pain level if the risk event does happen**

I fly small airplanes in the Pacific Northwest, and a constant concern for pilots in this region is ice. Water is pretty basic, but it can do weird things under the right conditions. The water droplets that make up clouds can become "supercooled," that is, they are colder than 32 degrees, but remain liquid. When an airplane disturbs these droplets, they break and immediately freeze to the plane's wings, propeller, windshield, and anything else sticking out into the airflow. This is BAD. The propeller that creates power is suddenly much less powerful, the wings that create lift suddenly create a lot less lift, and all that ice adds a substantial amount of weight that really makes the airplane want to just obey the laws of gravity and go toward the dirt. You must have exactly the right combination of temperature and cloud makeup for this to happen, so pilots can't tell if a cloud will produce ice on the airplane until they are actually flying through it.

To avoid this problem and avoid the risk, I could simply never fly through a cloud, but in the Seattle area that would mean that I wouldn't fly very often. Instead I need a plan to reduce the pain if it does happen. Some airplanes have heated propellers or other kinds of de-icing equipment to remove the ice from the airplane if it appears. For planes with no special equipment the pilot must have a plan in place in advance for what he or she is going to do if the airplane starts to pick up ice. Turn around, climb, descend—it is different for each mission, but the point is that in order to reasonably take the risk you should have a plan *in advance* that avoids the worst-case scenario if the risk goes against you.

Coming back down to earth, we see this principle in the practice of having cash savings equal to six months expenses so that if you lose your job you are not "on the street" the next month. You may be able to reduce the chance of getting fired by showing up on time and working hard, but there are reasons for losing your job that you just can't control. So you make a plan for what to do if that does happen. You will use the money in savings to get through the time it takes you to either find a new job or adjust your lifestyle accordingly.

The idea shows up again in risky investments. It has been said, "never gamble more than you can afford to lose," and it is good advice. I have no problem with some very high-risk/high-potential investments I have seen over the years, as long as the investors understand the risk and know exactly what they will do if it goes against them. When they put 5% of their portfolio into something high risk and can afford to lose it all, fine. When I see someone who is barely making ends meet and wants to put 80% of their holdings in such a thing I get very worried. It is clear they do not have a viable plan for what to do if the investment tanks.

**Action # 3: If you can't handle the potential downside by yourself, get help**

Some risks are just too big to effectively handle by yourself. You can certainly make a plan for rebuilding your house if it burns down and start saving all the money it would require to rebuild, but two problems pop up with this strategy. (1) The house could burn down anytime, long before you were able to save up the money to replace it, and (2) That much money could probably be used much more effectively to make your life *Better*. The answer is insurance.

Insurance is a pretty simple concept, but it sure does have an image problem! It works like this: We predict that only a few people within a group will be hit with a certain disaster. If everyone in the group puts a small amount of money into a fund, the total of the fund is big enough to take care of the few people that have the problem. From that simple concept grows fire insurance, life insurance, disability insurance, car insurance, and so forth. It starts to get complicated when each member of the group is more or less likely to have a problem and make a claim on the insurance funds.

Teenage boys are far more likely to have a car accident than their parents, so they have to pay more into the car insurance fund. Smokers are more likely to die prematurely, so they pay more for their life insurance. Because of all the lawsuits these days, doctors are more likely to have a malpractice claim, so their rates have gone up. People don't like being told they are high risk and must pay more, so insurance rubs them the wrong way. If you have a claim, you are glad you have the insurance, but many people that never have a claim feel cheated. They feel that they paid into the fund all those years and never got anything from it. In fact they did; they got a viable plan for dealing with the problem without having to keep large amounts of money sitting idle "just in case." But it doesn't really *feel* like they got anything, so it is easy to have a negative opinion. Don't fall into that trap. If you received peace of mind for your insurance dollars, you got your money's worth even if nothing happened to you. Really, would you rather be the person with the car wreck? No, what we want is to not pay the insurance AND have nothing bad happen. That's not realistic, so don't waste any mental energy being annoyed because it won't work for you.

The key to making your life *Better* in this area is to use the insurance to create a plan to deal with the disaster in a much more efficient way than you could all by yourself. By being more efficient with your resources, you leave more of them available to work on other aspects of making your life *Better*. You are also able to immediately eliminate the worry and stress of not having a plan, because most insurance is effective as soon as you sign up or perhaps after a very short waiting period. Insurance can work well for large losses, but don't go overboard, and be smart about what you are buying. Remember that there are many risks that are small, and you can handle those yourself. Make sure to avoid buying duplicate coverage. For example, let's suppose you have a car insurance policy that covers you in a rental car, and without thinking about it you sign up for the rental car company's coverage as well. Now you are paying twice for essentially the same coverage. There are times when you might want to do this on purpose, such as in a foreign country, but you should at least take the time to understand what you have and make an informed decision.

Bottom line on insurance: It is a great tool to be used in the right place, and it can put a contingency plan in place in one day that would take you years to create by yourself. It can be complicated and does take some time and energy to get right, but don't shy away from the right idea just because of the bad image insurance has.

## SUMMARY

1. Life isn't fair, and bad things do happen to good people.

2. In order to make your life *Better*, you need to look carefully at what your risks are and know what the worst case is, rather than just having a vague sense of worry all the time.

3. There are some risks you can choose whether to take or not. Consider if you really want to take them.

4. For the risks you do have, be sure you have a plan to deal with the problem if the worst happens.

5. For some risks you can put together a good contingency plan by yourself, but for many of the larger ones buying insurance makes a whole lot more sense.

You can use money to create security, but you can't eliminate all the risk in your life. Your life will be *Better* if you have clearly thought through what your risks are and what will happen if they go against you, and you have a plan for if they do.

# CHAPTER 6

# Saving money for future spending

## Keeping your money

There are many options for where to put the money you choose to keep. Some are very safe, others are risky, some have tax advantages, and there is always under the mattress if all else fails. As in the other areas we have discussed, there is not one right answer for everyone. In order to keep your money in a way that is *Better* for you, we need to rethink what might appear to be obvious. There are four big mistakes that I see all the time:

**Mistake #1: If I'm smart, I can see what's coming and get out just before everything goes down.**

There are lots of places to put your money, but from my experience nothing tweaks the general anxiety level for most people like "The Market." I meet a lot of people in my line of work. I also enjoy social dinners and have various groups that I see on a regular basis. There is one question that almost always comes up, no matter who I'm talking to: "What do you think 'The Market' is going to do?" I always have the same answer: "I don't know." No one is happy with this answer! In fact, most people hate it. They are sure that I do know but just don't want to tell them. The reality is that I believe that on a <u>long-term</u> basis the stock markets will continue to produce a good return, as they have for the last 100+ years, but in the short term (which is what everyone wants to know about) there is no reliable way to predict what "The Market" will do. By accepting that fact, I look at where to keep my money a little differently, and I sleep a whole lot better at night. But what about the huge number of news outlets dedicated to exploring what's going to happen in "The Market"?

There is a very deep-seated belief that if you just tried a little harder to understand, picked up a little more information from a great source, or got a tip that you and only you knew about, you could beat the system and secure financial wealth. There is some validity to the fact that good money managers do a great deal of research about an investment to really understand it before placing money there. It's called due diligence, and I'm all for it. But I also firmly believe that no one can predict the future with any accuracy. Even if I don't personally believe it is possible to predict the future, there is a multimillion dollar industry dedicated to people who do believe. There are magazines, webcasts, subscriptions, Twitter feeds, and probably some form of smoke signals that all purport to give you the information that no one else has so you can beat the system and sell everything the day before the market crashes. It just isn't that simple. There are so many factors that affect finances, such as bubbles, recessions, bull markets, sell-offs, inflation, a rising dollar, a falling dollar, tax increases, tax cuts, Republicans, Democrats, and so forth, and each of these factors interacts with the other factors and thousands of related factors to create what actually "happens." Even the "experts" don't agree. One of my favorite sayings around our industry is: "for every economist, there is an equal and opposing economist" (with apologies to Sir Isaac Newton).

Why do we devour all of those predictions? Unrealistic expectations. I know a man who has a business that launches products over the Internet. I asked him what sorts of products usually launch best, and his answer was simple: *dream* products—get rich in real estate with no money down, lose weight in 10 days while lying on the couch, cure your medical symptoms with a simple remedy first used by the ancient Aztecs, and so forth. The belief that there is a way to "beat the system" is certainly part of our cultural hardwiring, very much like the *More is Better* preconception.

I said earlier I don't know what the market is going to do, and, by accepting that fact, I look at where to keep my money a little differently. Because I acknowledge that I don't know what is going to happen, I only have one reasonable course of action, and that is diversification.

Here's a rather sad example. Back in 1999 during the dot-com boom, a couple in their late 20s came in to the office. They both worked at a very successful high-tech company, and they had about $4,000,000 worth of company stock and nothing else. I asked them how I could help, and they said, *"We have this great plan for our lives. We are going to retire early, we've found a piece of property we love, we have the house designed, John is going to follow his passion of music, Jane is going to teach computer skills for a while, then we are going to raise a family. We need to know if we have enough money to do that and how we get started."* I did all the analysis and came back to them with the answer. "Yes, you have enough money to do this, and the first step is to sell at least 80% of your company stock and diversify it to more conservative holdings. Your big risk now is having the funding for all these dreams go away." Their smiles went away. The mood in the room went dark. They said, *"You don't work with many young people do you? Everyone knows that if you are young you take lots of risk and, after all, our company stock doubled in the last 90 days!"* The meeting didn't last much longer. Sadly, neither did their portfolio balance. The bubble burst in early 2000, and with it went their ability to do all the things they wanted.

Was I so smart that I knew the bubble was going to burst? No. Was I telling them to sell because I had inside information that their company's stock was about to go over the falls? Again, no. I didn't know what was going to happen, but we don't live in a static world—the factors that affect the markets and investments are constantly changing and at an ever-increasing rate. By having everything in one place they were totally exposed to something happening and affecting everything they had. Rather than *predicting* what was going to happen, I wanted to *protect* them from whatever was going to happen. Had we diversified, their portfolio still would have gone down some, but they would have avoided the catastrophic loss they actually experienced. They effectively predicted a certain future, bet their entire net worth on it, and lost. Whether you want to take that sort of bet is up to you, but to make your life *Better* you should really understand what you are putting at risk and how often predicting the future really works.

## Mistake #2: Always dump the losers and buy what's hot

Because our financial world is dynamic and ever-changing, *something* is going to happen, and it will affect different investments in different ways. For example, if interest rates rise, my long-term bonds will go down in value since their interest rate is set for many years, but my bank stocks might go up because banks benefit from being able to charge consumers the higher rates more quickly. This is not a book about investment theory, so I won't get into a lot of the known causal relationships, but just know that many holdings act differently from each other in response to a common event. This is the key, so I'll repeat it in another way: any given financial market change will make one type of holding look more attractive and a different type of holding look less attractive. The fancy term for this concept is "negative correlation." The second key concept here is that markets tend to cycle, so that although one area is out of favor now, that won't always be the case. Your favorite holding now? Probably at some time over the next 10 years, it won't be.

Because of this negative correlation and the tendency of markets to cycle, in a well-diversified portfolio we should have a few holdings that are currently doing well and a few that are down in value. Now comes the part that can seem really counter-intuitive: from time to time, we should rebalance by selling some of the ones that are up and buying some of the ones that are down. Yes, you read that right, sell some of the winners. (This is what the couple I saw in 1999 should have done!) Use that money to buy other holdings that are down in value now, but will likely cycle back up over time. Don't go overboard; just come back to your original target balance for your portfolio diversification. This provides us some protection against the unknown future and gets us in a place to not worry about "What is the market going to do?" A nice side benefit with this method is that you often "sell high" and "buy low," which is certainly better than what many people do. They get frustrated a certain holding is down, sell it low, and put that money into their favorite, effectively "buying high." After a few repetitions of this, the portfolio is usually going nowhere and the investor is very frustrated. Not a recipe for *Better*.

Your biggest challenge with this approach is your emotions! It simply does not *feel* right to sell some of your winners and buy some of what currently looks like a loser. Resist this feeling. Don't let greed take you down the path of *More is Better*. Use your logic to make these decisions, not your emotions. Many people find that having an advisor to keep them on track is very helpful, because the advisor is more detached and thus more likely to stick to the plan. One caveat on when to adjust the portfolio is taxes: sometimes there is a better or worse time to buy or sell something because of tax implications, and, as mentioned before, we do want to be paying attention to keeping our taxes as low as legally possible.

## Mistake #3: More risk is better; it means more return

Most people are comfortable with the fact that there is a trade-off between risk and potential return. There is a common misconception that for every unit of risk you get a unit of reward, and, if you have a lot of time, you can wait out any risk. In reality it doesn't work that way.

If you start at a point of no risk and no return and want to move up the scale a bit, you get a good deal more potential return by taking a *little* more risk. From there, for the next few steps, you seem to get about an equal amount of additional return for the extra risk you take. Then, a strange thing happens. For each step toward the higher risk options, you take a much greater risk and only get a tiny amount of additional potential return. We call this diminishing returns, and for most people it doesn't make a lot of sense.

You don't have to limit yourself to just one holding with its inherent risk characteristics. By mixing different investments you can create a blend that has the risk level you are comfortable with, and the risk from one investment can help offset the risk from another, making the whole blend more stable. What's the right mix for you? A financial advisor can help with the technical details, but, before you go see one, go back to your Four Foundation statements that we developed in Chapter 3 and your plans for risk in Chapter 5.

If you love stability and fear the balance of your accounts ever going down, then your allocation should be very conservative. If you want the potential rewards that come from taking a big risk, are comfortable with that risk, and know exactly what you will do if that risk turns against you, then a more aggressive approach might be called for. Rather than fall into the *More is Better* trap, consider the level of risk you can accept and the level of return that you need. Compare these levels to your Four Foundations of making your life *Better*. Be aware that you may need to compromise, either by accepting some additional risk or by reducing your needs so that everything balances. The goal is to be intentional when defining where you keep your money and the risk/reward trade-offs of the strategy you choose. If you can do that, you will be much more likely to have a *Better* experience.

## Mistake # 4: This is easy, I'll just do it myself

Now that you have an idea what you might want for your holdings, there is the operational problem of getting your portfolio put in place and looked after over time. There are some great investment professionals in your hometown, and I would recommend using one, unless one of your great loves in life is managing money. As I mentioned before, there is a benefit to having a detached third party to keep you on track, and the concept of hiring help to free up your time and energy for doing the things you love certainly applies here.

What type of advisor is right for you? Consider what you want and what will make your life *Better*. Consider how advisors' services fit with what you need, rather than who is cheapest or who has the best marketing.

Referrals from friends are a great place to start, but your friend's definition of *Better* may be different from yours. Interview the advisor and be sure the person you work with really understands your goals. Because most people default to the *More is Better* notion, many of these well-intentioned professionals are not used to any goals other than simply *More*. Often they will assume that is what you want unless you tell them otherwise. You will be far happier with the end results if you know what to expect and if both of you are working toward the same end result.

Since you are exchanging some of your money for help, make sure that you clearly understand the advisor's compensation structure. As we talked about in Chapter 4 on spending, you want to be comfortable that the exchange is going to make your life *Better*. Ideally your advisor should be compensated in a manner that is in line with your goals for the portfolio. This can be tricky with commission product reps if your goals are to spend down the portfolio for retirement income or if you want maximum security but not much growth. Fee-only planners can sometimes be more flexible on this point, but they tend to get paid to create the plan, not on how well it works. Often a good solution is a combination of both—fee-only for the overall advice you need, and commission or percentage for product-related help.

No matter who helps with the basic strategy, asset allocation, and product placement, it is worth your time to understand what you own and who is actually making the operational decisions on a day-to-day basis. If you put money in almost anything besides an old mason jar, somebody else is making some decisions regarding how that money is used, and that somebody will need to get paid. Choices such as mutual funds, managed accounts, cash values in life insurance, company stocks, CDs at the bank, or funds inside your 401(k), all have management teams to make the decisions on how your money will be used. How much risk they take, which company's stock they buy, how diversified their bonds are, whether they buy sub-prime loans, whether they have any screens about the type of businesses they will invest in, and what they charge are good pieces of information to have to help you understand how they think.

What you are really doing is hiring that team for their *judgment*. Because no one ever truly knows what is coming in the way of markets, economies, interest rates, and so forth, we really are hiring a team to take us into uncharted waters. For my money, I want a team with a solid amount of experience, and that experience should show consistent, excellent judgment over a long period of time, not just one super year that makes up for nine lousy ones. You don't have to spend all your time digesting tons of minutiae if that isn't for you, but by making sure you have a team that you can believe in running your money, you end up with a portfolio that is *Better* for you.

## SUMMARY

1. You need to have realistic expectations about investments and markets. There is no secret formula out there for all gain and no risk.

2. Rebalance investments the right way, by trimming what is up and adding to what is down.

3. More risk does not necessarily mean more return. The two are linked, but there is definitely a point of diminishing returns. Know what risk/reward profile is *Better* for you.

4. Unless managing money is your dream job, find someone to help. Be sure that they have a long history of good judgment and that they really understand what *Better* means to you.

Start by knowing what makes the place where you keep your money *Better* for you. Have realistic expectations about what is likely to happen and then relax and let it happen. The stress will be less and life will be *Better*.

# CHAPTER 7

# Paying money to taxes

Pay all the taxes you legally owe and not one penny more. That sounds simple enough, but the reality is that our tax system has become very complex. Every locality is different, but most people pay some form of property tax, sales tax, income tax, social security tax, excise tax, estate tax, and value-added tax. Because the systems overlap each other and are administered on federal, state, and local levels it gets very confusing, and the temptation is to just throw your hands up and pay whatever is asked. Resist this temptation!

In Chapter 2 we reviewed the court case in which the judge wrote in his decision that a prudent person would arrange his or her affairs so that his or her taxes would be as low as possible. If you don't do that, then you are choosing to give some extra money to the government. Getting tax rules all figured out takes some diligence on your part, and for some people the time it takes to be that diligent just doesn't seem worth the effort, so they pay more in taxes than they have to. But, really, they are *choosing* to give that extra amount so that they don't have to be bothered with keeping records and understanding how the tax laws work or hiring a CPA.

It might be a little easier if the tax laws stayed the same, but they do not, and in fact they change very rapidly. Because tax laws do change so frequently, a sound strategy for saving taxes in the future is "tax diversification." This is where you have your holdings spread out among various accounts and products that traditionally are taxed *differently*. For many years life insurance, muni bonds, stocks, government bonds, annuities, IRAs and Roth IRAs have all been taxed in a manner unique to that account/product. As tax laws change over time, one type of account might become more favorable to draw from than another. By having several "buckets" that are all taxed differently, you can choose to draw from the one that is most tax favorable at the time.

In addition to having accounts that are taxed differently, for most of us there is some "low hanging fruit" that you can take advantage of with minimal effort. Company retirement plans, tax-deductible interest on home loans, tax-free growth of certain college savings plans, and the tax advantages of life insurance are currently some of the more basic opportunities for reducing your taxes, assuming that the underlying product is something that makes sense for you. Quite often I see people who bought products that were meant to be great tax breaks but were totally unsuitable for their overall situations. Since taxes are a "hot button" for most of us, it is pretty easy to get drawn into a bad investment when it is promoted for its tax benefits, so be sure the product/ strategy makes sense for you first.

One of the easiest ways to reduce taxes, in my opinion, is charitable giving. If you itemize deductions on your tax return, under current law the IRS will allow you a deduction against your taxable income for most charitable gifts. It is not a $1 for $1 credit—you can't avoid all your taxes by giving the same amount of money to your favorite charity. In addition, there are some limits regarding public and private charities that are beyond the scope of this book. However, within limits, a gift to a charity usually reduces the income tax you owe. When it comes to estate taxes, the effect is even greater because the limits are much less restrictive.

Your last will and testament can save a lot of money in taxes. Because your estate could owe tax when you die and this tax is determined in part by who you left your estate to, the contents of your will have a profound impact on how much tax your estate will pay. The same is true for the beneficiary statements on your retirement plans, life insurance, and annuities. If you either have no will at all, or a simple "I leave everything to my spouse" will, and your estate is over certain limits, a new will could save your beneficiaries a large amount of tax. These laws are changing almost daily as I write this, so I will not go into specific strategies, but suffice it to say that if your net worth is over one million dollars and you have a simple will you should discuss the issue with your financial advisor, accountant or attorney.

Next come the more sophisticated concepts, and the tax avoidance/tax evasion slope gets slippery in a hurry. If you are the sort of person that likes to play tough with the IRS, who doesn't mind regular audits and the occasional lawsuit, and who knows what to do if you lose, you might make your life *Better* by pursuing these aggressive tactics. You will need to find a good CPA and tax attorney to explore your situation and see what applies to you and make your decisions about what you are comfortable with using your decision model from Chapter 3. In no case would I ever recommend that you do anything aggressive as a "do-it-yourself" project. Every year there is something new on the Internet about an off-shore tax haven or declaring your 40 acres in the woods to be a sovereign nation. Don't be fooled; these schemes are always a bad idea.

Even if you don't go super-aggressive from a legal standpoint, you can take this way too far and easily get on the wrong side of *Better*. I frequently hear that clients want to do something that is legal but just plain nutty, because they believe it will save them "a bundle on taxes." Good goal, but at what cost? People talk about getting divorced after 25 years in a happy marriage in order to be able to file separate returns, buying cars they don't want because there is a tax incentive, or selling an investment at a loss to offset gains even though the investment has a very bright future. Getting too caught up in tax avoidance can lead to decisions that actually decrease your quality of life. Decisions you make about your finances should be driven by what makes your life *Better*, not a static goal of "fewer taxes."

The goal is to pay enough attention to your taxes without going overboard. If paying attention to taxes really isn't your thing, go back and reread Chapter 4 (the section about the joys of hiring help) and then find a good CPA. My experience is that working with a professional or using a detailed software program and paying attention is always worth the effort/money when it comes to taxes. You may have to walk a fine line between "arranging your affairs so that your taxes shall be as low as possible," and not doing things that reduce your quality of life. But when you find that balance, life gets *Better*.

## SUMMARY

1. Tax systems are complex, overlapping, and constantly changing.

2. "Tax diversification" can give you tax saving options when you need to take money out of accounts.

3. There are time-tested, basic strategies to reduce taxes that everyone can follow with minimal effort.

4. Correct beneficiary designations and the correct will can reduce estate taxes for your family.

5. You can go too far with tax avoidance and end up reducing your quality of life.

Do your best to legally avoid taxes without getting so caught up in the process that you reduce your quality of life. Less tax is a good goal, but ultimately, *Better is Better*.

# CHAPTER 8

# Giving money to help others

If I gave you a million dollars and said that you had to give it away to charity, who would you give it to and why?

Stop for a minute and try to answer that question; it's not as easy as you might think. When you ponder giving in those terms, it changes the starting point for giving. We are so used to responding to a single request with either a "yes" or "no" that we don't think about where we would give if it were just up to us. Each of us has charitable causes that resonate with us for a variety of reasons. If someone close to you died of breast cancer, you are likely to support a friend participating in the Susan G. Komen Foundation's annual Race for the Cure. If you love classical music, you might give to your local symphony. If you went through the Boy/Girl Scouts as a child, you can probably be convinced to give to that organization as an adult. From what I see, for the most part people simply respond to charitable requests. They are reactive rather than being proactive. Very few people I have talked to seem to have any sort of plan to be intentional about their giving. To make our giving *Better*, we have to change that.

First, decide on how much you want to give for the entire year. There is no right answer as to the amount, but I believe it is important to sit down by yourself and/or with your partner to decide, in advance, what you can afford and what makes the most sense for you to give. Many people have different methods for this. Some look at how much they need to live and give a portion of what's left over. Others really like to push themselves and try to always give more than last year. Many churches recommend giving 10% of your income. Whatever the method, be sure to consider that you have two currencies you can give: money and time.

You may not have much extra money in your budget at this point, but maybe you have extra time to give. This is especially true of retired people and parents who stay at home during the day when their kids are at school. On the other hand, you may not have one spare minute, but a solid discretionary cash flow. Either way, when you come up with your amount to give for the year, express it in dollars and in time, such as: "I/we will give _____ dollars and _____ hours this year." How you come up with the numbers and what form they take (hours or dollars) is your choice, but come up with a target for the year and write it down. Until it is on paper, it is just a thought. On page 88 I have an example of a worksheet that will help you put these ideas down on paper in an organized way. You can find a blank worksheet on my website: www.jamescrichards.com

Next, list the three most important areas of giving for you. You can go back to your Four Foundations from Chapter 3 and look at the issues that are meaningful to you. This will give you some guidance, but there may be issues that are meaningful to you that do not translate into your personal wants/needs/fears. You may not personally worry about having enough food to eat but still feel very strongly about working on world hunger. This is a place where the more effort you put in, the better the result. At this point you should identify three broad categories, not three specific charities.

If you want, you can add some structure to your charitable giving plan by, for example, giving no more than a set amount for Category 1 charities or only using your company's match program to benefit your Category 2 charities. You can make this as simple or as complicated as you like, but when you are done you have a nice guideline for what you want your charitable money to accomplish. This will make your giving decisions much easier.

Now you can review specific requests with much more clarity. Are they in one of your three broad categories? If so, decide whether you think they further *your* goals and how much you want to give to them. You no longer need to dread the call from the school foundation! If one of your areas was your children's education, then, yes, you will give. By looking at your guidelines, you know how much you can give, and whether you will apply your company's match. This works great when the charities come looking for you, but if one of your areas of giving is one that you have not given to before you will need to do a little research, and the Internet is a great resource for this. As of this writing, www.charitynavigator.org and www.charitywatch.org are two sources that will get you started, but there are many more. You can also find some information on the website of the charity that you are considering, although this may be somewhat biased.

While we are on the subject of evaluating charities, I want to touch on the concept of leverage. This is where you look at a problem, try to identify the point at which the trouble starts, and then support a charity that is working on the root cause rather than just the symptoms.

For example, there is a lot of evidence that money is far more productive when spent on early childhood learning than on trying to change the behavior of errant 19-year-olds. If you get to an at-risk kid early and keep some of the problems from ever happening, the result is a citizen who not only does not need support later on in life but instead has a job, pays taxes, gives to other charities, and becomes part of the solution, rather than part of the problem. This is just one example, but, for every issue meaningful to you, there are ways to give that are more "end result" productive than others. Generally it does not take an immense amount of effort to figure out which ones they are, and by focusing your giving on the area that makes the most difference you end up with a *Better* result.

Another great option is to "hire help" in the form of a foundation or broad-based organization. With this approach, you give to a group that does research into the best way to distribute charitable dollars in the area you are concerned about. The group then supports the individual organizations that are actually "in the trenches." Take a careful look at the group's history and perform some due diligence before making your contribution. Once you are satisfied that it acts in a way you approve of, you can write one check and be done.

Here's an example of how I might lay out a charitable giving plan:

**The Better is Better Approach**
**Charitable Giving Worksheet**

Calendar Year ___**2011**___

During this year I/we want to give ___**$20,000**___ Dollars and ___**50**___ Hours

| Category #1<br>**Early childhood<br>learning and support** | | Category #2<br>**Supporting people<br>who want to work** | | Category #3<br>**Environmental<br>or climate concerns** | |
|---|---|---|---|---|---|
| **Dollars Target**<br>$10,000 | **Hours Target**<br>20 | **Dollars Target**<br>$6,000 | **Hours Target**<br>0 | **Dollars Target**<br>$4,000 | **Hours Target**<br>30 |
| **Dollars so far**<br>$4,500 | **Hours so far**<br>10 | **Dollars so far**<br>$3,000 | **Hours so far**<br>0 | **Dollars so far**<br>$1,000 | **Hours so far**<br>10 |
| Use company match? **Yes** | | Use company match? **No** | | Use company match? **No** | |
| Potential charities to consider | | | | | |
| – Eastside Preschool<br>– Foster care center<br>– Early readers program<br>– Family shelter | | – Re-training Alliance<br>– Microlending partners<br>– Community college tech<br>  for adults program | | – Recycle effort at school<br>– Volunteer to remove ivy<br>  at local park<br>– Bike to work outreach<br>  program | |

Now that you have your targets, keep track. I do this by maintaining a paper file folder that stores all requests for charity as well as my worksheet of how much I will give and what broad categories I choose to support. Once a quarter, my wife and I sit down and review what is in the file. We make decisions on what to support and how much to contribute. This quarterly task is very easy to complete because we have our guidelines already established. The worksheet also allows us to keep track of our giving over the year, check that we are giving the amounts we planned on, and be sure that an area we care about hasn't been neglected. This approach also has a nice side benefit, and that is the freedom to say "No." When you know what your target is and something doesn't fit, you can just politely decline the request and feel good about it.

## SUMMARY

1. Decide in advance how much time and money you want to give to charities each year.

2. Write out what broad themes you want to support and how much time and money you want to give to each of them.

3. Use your written guidelines to evaluate requests and see if they align with your giving program.

4. Keep track of your giving and enjoy the knowledge that you made a difference.

Giving to charities in an intentional fashion causes you to feel good about what you have done, gives you the ability to say "no" without guilt, and reduces your taxes. What a great combination for making your life *Better*.

# Summary points

My goal with this book was to share some of what I have learned during my 20 years as a financial advisor and to encourage you to think about the way you make your financial decisions, because they have such a direct connection to your quality of life. I tried to do this in a quick and entertaining fashion, so that the reader stayed engaged at the conceptual level and did not get bogged down in minutiae. But life is hectic and even a quick read like this can get interrupted, so here is a summary of the main points that I hope you can keep in mind and use to your benefit.

- Realize that we have a default decision model and it may not take us where we want to go. Remember that *More* is not always *Better*; *Better is Better.*

    - *Better* is a personal concept; yours is unique to you
    - All the financial decisions we make have an effect on our quality of life

- Finances are complicated, but we can simplify down to five main categories:

  - **Spend it** on basic needs, possessions, experiences, and help
  - Both **Spend and Save it** to create security
  - **Save it** for a future spending need
  - **Give it** to the government by paying taxes
  - **Give it** to charity

- Figure out what *Better* means to you and build your decision model (the Four Foundations) based on four core emotions:

  - What I Love
  - What I Hate
  - What I Want
  - What I Fear

- Use that decision model to make decisions about the five categories of things you can do with your money.

- How are you going to spend it?

  - Possessions
  - Experiences
  - Help

- How much security do you want?
  - Savings
  - Insurance

- What future spending do you need to save for?
  - Retirement
  - Big-ticket items
  - Opportunity fund

- How are you going to pay the minimum tax required?

  - Pay attention and understand the system
  - Don't go overboard with extreme strategies

- What is the best way to give some of it away?
  - Be intentional
  - Use time as well as money

- Remember *More* is not always *Better*;

  ### *Better is Better*